The Legendary Land

To
James D Cox
on the occasion of the
3rd Asia Pacific Economic
Law Forum
Christchurch 1997

REED

The Lege

Morning light, Glendhu Bay, Lake Wanaka.

ndary Land

Text by Witi Ihimaera
Photographs by Holger Leue

with a foreword by Keri Hulme

For my parents, Günther and Marga Leue.
— H.L.

For Jessica and Olivia Ihimaera-Smiler and the generation that will inherit the legendary land.
— W.I.

Published in 1994 by Reed Books, a division of Reed Publishing (NZ) Ltd, 39 Rawene Road, Birkenhead, Auckland. Associated companies, branches and representatives throughout the world.

This book is copyright. Except for the purpose of fair reviewing, no part of this publication may be reproduced or transmitted in any form or by any means, electronic or mechanical, including photocopying, recording, or any information storage and retrieval system, without permission in writing from the publisher. Infringers of copyright render themselves liable to prosecution.

Text copyright © Witi Ihimaera and Reed Publishing 1994
Photographs copyright © Reed Publishing 1994

ISBN 0 7900 0373 2 casebound edition
ISBN 0 7900 0374 0 slipcase edition

Project coordinator: Ian Watt
Editor: Susan Brierley
Cover and text design: Chris Lipscombe
Text set in Bauer Bodoni.
Film separations by Star Graphics, Auckland.
Printing and binding by Everbest Printing Co, Hong Kong.

Contents

Foreword 6

Prologue 9

The Story of the Land 12

The People of the Land 18

Te Reinga to Auckland 24

Waikato to the Volcanic Plateau 50

Coromandel to the Wairarapa 70

Taranaki to Wellington 96

Nelson and Marlborough to Kaikoura 110

Christchurch and Canterbury 126

The West Coast 150

Dunedin and Otago 170

Murihiku: The South 196

Epilogue 220

Photographic Notes 222

Acknowledgements 222

Foreword
by Keri Hulme

We are sitting round a new table, here in my octagon in the Free Republic of Okarito. We are celebrating the table indeed, its advent and its beauty. Smooth, richly figured planks of rimu have been so cunningly knit together the joins are invisible. While it is rectangular, its subtle curves echo the roundish room. It is long and wide enough for eight people to be entertained. There are only three of us at the moment — myself (a writer, a fisher, a painter — though 'dreamer' is probably the best label); my next-door neighbour Judith Maloney, who is a weaver, and the table's maker, Richard Waller. Richard is from Germany, and trained in all aspects of woodwork there, but Okarito lured him away, and he is now resident here.

We are drinking Lindauer (a New Zealand sparkling wine named after the artist Gottfried Lindauer, who was also from Germany) and eating succulent Nelson scallops that Judith has cooked Cajun-style, spiced and seared black on the outside, sweetly raw at the centre. We are happy, a bit rowdy, laughing and singing and caressing my new table … and there's a knock at the door.

He looks a little perturbed, this young man with the rimless glasses and observant eyes, but he has an air of gentleness, quizzicality. Holger Leue, a photographer, he murmurs, I don't want to intrude. So we invite him to wet the table's head.

There are links between Okarito and Germany aside from tables and wines. Some of my fiction has been translated into German, and I get a lot of letters from German readers. There is a youth hostel here, famous among people in Frankfurt and Cologne. Okarito has a powerful though ascetic beauty, and many hundred backpackers from Germany visit the place yearly. Holger is another visitor.

But one with a difference: many of our visitors take things away with them — shells and stones and driftwood; congenial memories of local hospitality and bonfires on the beach, the still silver lagoon, gull cries, the rumbustious

The Legendary Land

Keri Hulme — writer, fisher, painter, 'dreamer' — on the beach at Okarito.

ocean, kotuku, and the long, people-free, ironsand beaches. Not many visitors bring gifts back.

Leue's photography reminds me most of Robin Morrison's work. There is a similar deft focusing on quirky detail, balanced by a holistic approach to the landscape — people and buildings and vehicles have their place as well as mountains and water. An obvious love of the beautiful scene is countered by cunning snaps of the offbeat, the compellingly ugly. There is, however, an essential difference between the two photographers: Morrison was a New Zealander, and lived here for much of his too-short life. While Leue has visited often, he sees the land and its people with a discerning, insightful but foreign eye.

And that is his offering to readers everywhere: that is his gift back to us here in Aotearoa.

Kia ora na
Keri Hulme

Prologue

The Legendary Land

When Maui went fishing with his brothers and dragged Aotearoa from the sea, the first part of the land to broach the surface was Mount Hikurangi, on the East Coast of the North Island.

As the mountain reared out of the waves the force of the water bore Maui's canoe, *Nukutaimehameha*, down the slope. Suddenly the canoe became caught in a cleft of the mountain, coming to rest upside down in a small lake of water that had been trapped by the rising of the mountain from the sea. Even today, when the air vibrates with psychic energy the sails and broken bailer of Maui's waka can still be seen. Hikurangi is our Mount Ararat and Maui's canoe is our Noah's Ark.

Every day of every year since the time of Maui, Hikurangi has been the first point on the Earth's surface to be touched by the finger of the sun.

It is a compass point for our world.

A point by which, if one is lost or navigating the expanse of space, one's position can be fixed.

A flash of light.

There and mark. Aotearoa.

The legendary land.

Aotearoa New Zealand

Volcanic landscape, White Island, Bay of Plenty.

The Legendary Land

Ka to he ra, ka rere he ra.

A sun sets, a day is born, no sooner is one day over than another begins.

The Story of the Land

Kingdom of the Gods

Aotearoa, or New Zealand, has always been blessed by the gods. The blessings, however, have not been without struggle. Even before Maui's time, at the very beginning of Everything, our legacy was hard won.

They say, for instance, that when Rangi the Sky Father and Papa the Earth Mother came spinning out of Chaos, the cosmic generator from which all life originated, they were wrapped so tightly in each other's arms and legs that their children were born within the confines of this embrace and could not find room to stand up. There were seventy such children. Among them were Tane Mahuta, god of the forest; Tangaroa, god of the ocean; Rongo ma Tane, god of the kumara plant; Tu Matauenga, god of man and war; Haumia Tiketike, god of the fern root; Ruaumoko, god of earthquakes; and Tawhirimatea, god of wind and storms.

Led by Tane, twenty-eight of the children began to plot to separate their parents. Being male, they considered murder. But Tawhirimatea argued against this parricide. So one by one, over aeons of Time, the god children attempted to separate their parents using other methods. One by one they failed, until Tane Mahuta, with his hands placed firmly on his Earth Mother, kicked with his feet against his Sky Father.

It was a lucky kick. Or perhaps it was Destiny.

A gap.

A crack of light.

The light came flooding in.

Of course there was an aftermath. Both Rangi and Papa kept reaching for each other, and whenever the god children were able to prise their hands apart the parents would find another grip.

It was Tane who then ordered the arms of the primal parents to be chopped off. The red glow in the sky is the Sky Father's blood. The red ochre in the earth is the Earth Mother's blood.

The outcome was torrential weeping, mist, snow and hail. Some say this was the Maori version of the great Flood.

Again the order was given, this time for the Earth Mother to be turned over so that she and the Sky Father would never see each other again.

This is often the way of children trying to make their own way in the world. The anger over the bloodiness of the separation, however, is still expressed by those gods who were not in favour of it. Tawhirimatea expresses his rage in storms that lash our country. And Ruaumoko, who went into the belly of his mother when she was turned, still rumbles his earthquake warning.

The Coming of Mankind

Tane, who coordinated the separation of the primal parents, was a very clever god. He could see that without Woman he and his brother gods would not have children. Indeed, we are told that the god children had often pondered the subject of producing a non-godlike race of descendants to take possession of the world. The god children realised that such a woman would have to be born of earth.

Tane therefore instructed the Earth Mother to fashion such a woman. This first Eve was named Hine Ahuone.

Now, all this does not imply that Woman was of lower estate than Man, for Man had not yet been born. Assuredly both Woman and Man were lower than the gods but, in the sequence of things, the gods created Woman first. Man came later.

Again it was Tane who, in mating with Hine Ahuone, created the new race of mankind. Their first-born was a daughter, and Tane mated with her also. Her name was Hine Titama, woman of the dawn. It was she who, through the shame of that first incest, fled to the Underworld and found her destiny as Hine nui te Po, the great Mother Death who claims us all.

This was the same Mother Death whom Maui, who came much later in the story of the world, sought to challenge in a feat of somewhat doubtful biology. Maui the trickster, he was called, Maui the bold and impudent one. And what did he plan to do? Why, to enter between Hine nui te Po's thighs, make his way through her body, and reappear at her mouth. Maui took some of the small birds of the forest with him, including the fantail. 'But don't laugh,' he told them, 'otherwise the old lady will wake up.'

By this time Hine nui te Po had grown old and formidable. Her body was human but her eyes were greenstone, her hair was sea-kelp and her mouth was like a barracouta. She lived in the direction of the red light in the western sky.

Maui told the birds, 'Sshhh.'

He crept up between Hine nui te Po's legs. His head began to disappear.

The fantail couldn't help but laugh.

Hine nui te Po awoke.

She closed her thighs.

Maui suffered the pangs of the First Death.

Thus began the Twilight of the Gods.

Maui, The Superhero

But Maui did not die in vain. Before his death his achievements had secured him a place in history. His whole life has the stature of a fabulous epic, a Wagnerian Ring, although it began in horrendous circumstances.

Maui's mother, Taranga, had borne many children before Maui. When the pangs of Maui's birth began, she was alarmed because he was coming much too early. She believed he was stillborn.

Taranga grieved and, as was the manner in those days, cut her hair, placed the foetus Maui in it and cast him into the sea. He was swept to the beach, all tangled up in seaweed, and would have faced certain death from swarming flies and diving gulls, were it not for the god Rangi who rescued him and brought him up to have supernatural powers.

When he was older, Maui searched for Taranga. When he found her she did not, of course, recognise him. He joined his dancing brothers and, when Taranga saw him, she asked, 'Who are you?' He answered, 'I am Maui tikitiki a Taranga, the one whom you wrapped in your hair and threw into the sea.'

Maui's supernatural powers enabled him to accomplish many astounding feats. He turned his brother-in-law into a dog. He stole his grandmother's jawbone. He obtained fire. He encouraged his brothers to set a snare for the sun, which was going too fast across the sky, and in return for setting the sun free obtained its promise that it would go slower. Were it not for Maui, we would not have twenty-four-hour days.

However, as in most stories of younger brothers returning home, Maui's older brothers soon became jealous of him. On that fateful day when they went

The Legendary Land

fishing they decided to go without him. But Maui sneaked on board the canoe and only revealed himself when they were far out to sea.

When Maui fished up Aotearoa, using blood from his nose to bait his magic hook and chanting a powerful karakia, there was no doubt that the fish would be wondrous. Even Maui's brothers were in awe of it, although that did not stop them from hacking at it in their hunger and making of it a rugged landscape.

In its final death throes the fish reared up and caught Maui's canoe, *Nukutaimehameha*, within the lake on sacred Hikurangi mountain.

And we are back to the beginning of our story.

The first of many morning lights touched Hikurangi. The fish of Maui turned into stone.

A flash of light.

The land, already legendary, was waiting.

Soon, Man came.

Aotearoa New Zealand

Fern fronds, Haast Pass.

The Legendary Land

He pai te mahi ahakoa hu.

You can do good work
without making a noise.

The People of the Land

Vikings of the Sunrise

Some people say that when Maui fished up Aotearoa there were already tangata whenua, people of the land, on it. Others say that the first people did not arrive until much later.

These canoe voyagers were Polynesians. Thousands of years before, they had populated the northern Pacific. From the navel of Tonga and Samoa and then Raiatea in the Society Islands, they went eastward to Rapanui or Easter Island, northward to Hawaii, and finally south-westward down to Aotearoa, the southernmost point of what is known as the Polynesian triangle.

Maori call this ancestral place of origin Hawaiki.

It cannot be found on any map.

It is, like our land, legendary.

A man by the name of Kupe is generally credited with the discovery of New Zealand. His wife, Hine te aparangi, looked to the horizon and cried, 'He ao! He ao! A cloud! A cloud!'

Hence Aotearoa, the Land of the Long White Cloud.

Kupe took news of Aotearoa back to Hawaiki. Most people agree that a series of canoe voyages followed between AD 700 and 1000.

The voyages of the canoes have all the stuff of romance. Take the *Takitimu*, for instance. It was escorted by a school of fish, with a taniwha or monster named Ruamano ahead, and another named Arai te uru behind. The god Kahukura, taking the form of a rainbow, led the way by day, and by night the guide was a lunar halo. When the *Takitimu* struck rough weather the sacred axes with which the waka had been made chopped a way through the waves.

Not all the voyagers came by conventional means. Some tribes, like the Ngati Porou, proudly proclaim that their ancestor arrived riding on the back of a whale. Others claim a bird. After all, these were the times when there was no separation between man and god, when such things were possible.

Aotearoa was the last of the islands to be populated by these intrepid voyagers. This makes the Maori, the people of New Zealand, the youngest of the Polynesians.

They have all the boldness of their ancestor Maui, and all the magic of the potiki, the youngest.

They are the magic mokopuna, the bold grandchildren, of Polynesia.

Ships from the North

The coming of the first Europeans is also enshrouded in magic. There are stories of lost Spanish caravels and red-haired visitors from the stars.

The first documented arrival, however, occurred on 13 December 1642 when Abel Tasman finally found what he thought was the Great Southern Land. Such a land, so philosophers argued, must surely exist to balance the lands of the Northern Hemisphere. And in such a land, they reasoned, surely must reside riches beyond imagination.

Tasman named the place Staten Landt, and then Nieuw Zeeland. But after blood was spilt between his crew and local Maori, and finding no riches, he sailed away.

The British were the next to search for the Great Southern Land and thereby to discover New Zealand again. This time it was James Cook, who sighted the country in October 1769, and went on to circumnavigate the coast. Again, blood was spilt. And again, no riches were found. The perception of a Great Southern Land faded and the reality of New Zealand became established.

And what did the Maori think of these strangers?

'They took the ship at first for a gigantic bird, and were struck with the beauty and size of its wings, as they supposed the sails to be. But on seeing a smaller bird, unfledged, descending into the water, and a number of parti-coloured beings, apparently in human shape, the bird was regarded as a houseful of divinities.'

Not for long. Close inspection and violence from the strangers soon attested to their malevolence and 'it was therefore agreed that ... the sooner their society was dismissed, the better for the general welfare.'

For a time no colonial power claimed New Zealand. The British, however, indicated an interest by providing jurisdiction from New South Wales,

Aotearoa New Zealand

Australia. The French were interested also. However, it was primarily settlement plans for the colonies, coupled with missionary pressure and protestations that law and order should be established in New Zealand, which led to the signing of a Treaty at Waitangi, on 6 February 1840, between some Maori chiefs and representatives of the British Crown. The Treaty was supposed to establish partnership and guarantee indigenous rights to land, fisheries and culture. Instead, it established British sovereignty over the Maori people.

A Clash of Cultures

From the 1840s settlers began streaming to New Zealand, undaunted by promises made in the Treaty. In some quarters, the Treaty was regarded as giving the Government of the time licence to sell Maori land.

At Wairau in the South Island, twenty-two Europeans were killed in a clash between a survey party and the Maori chief Te Rauparaha. At Kororareka in the Far North, Hone Heke, in repeated acts of defiance, cut down the British flagstaff four times, the last time in 1845. For the next thirty years there was fighting between the two races, called 'fire in the fern' because no sooner was the fire extinguished in one area than it broke out somewhere else. The skirmishes culminated in a period of land wars, notably from 1863 to 1888.

A campaign of skirmishes developed in 1860–61 over the sale of a block of land at Waitara, in Taranaki. In 1863, war again broke out over an adjacent coastal block called Tataraimaka.

In 1853 the Maori people of the Waikato area, resenting secret land purchases, formed a loose confederation of tribes under a Maori king, King Potatau. When European troops crossed the northern Waikato boundary in 1863 war began, culminating in the battle of Orakau Pa in 1864. The British called for the Maori pa defenders to surrender. The reply was 'Ka whawhai tonu matou, ake, ake, ake!' 'We shall fight on forever and ever.'

The Bay of Plenty was the next area of conflict and Gate Pa its major battle arena. Then fire flared again in Taranaki. A new religion called Paimarire, or Hauhau, had arisen, founded by the prophet Te Ua. New courage was brought to the fighting, which continued under the command of the chief Titokowaru.

On the East Coast, Te Kooti Arikirangi began a campaign of astonishing brilliance. After being wrongfully imprisoned, he escaped and led an attack on the military settlement at Matawhero on 9 November 1868. Te Kooti was pursued by soldiers for many years before being pardoned. In later life he became the founder of the Ringatu Church.

The Legendary Land

Back in Taranaki, colonial forces marched on the Maori settlement of Parihaka, where they were met by little children singing and skipping, led by Te Whiti o Rongomai, a prophet and advocate of passive resistance.

At the height of the period of conflict there were ten British regiments stationed in New Zealand. Three million acres of land were confiscated.

Today, the Waitangi Tribunal adjudicates disputes between Maori and the New Zealand Government. As late as 1990, the Reverend Whakahuihui Vercoe, on behalf of the Maori people, felt compelled to say in the presence of Her Majesty Queen Elizabeth II on the Treaty grounds at Waitangi, 'You have still not honoured the Treaty.'

Magic Mokopuna

New Zealanders are today increasingly finding their identity as a country in and of the South Pacific. As well, more and more people from places other than Hawaiki or England have made New Zealand their home. In the process, they have transformed the land of our forefathers.

They have brought gifts of heritage from their own cultures. The riches of China, of Europe, of what was once known as the Soviet Union. The bounty of the New World, America and Canada. The excitement of the lands circling the Pacific Rim — Korea, Hong Kong, Singapore, Vietnam — from our closest neighbour Australia and the islands which lie within the great Pacific Ocean. Latterly, from the African continent.

They have come for many reasons. Some to escape from war-torn pasts. Some to make money. Others to fulfil long-held dreams and hopes. Some to take. Others to contribute. In the process we have become transformed. Not always in good or positive ways, but generally we have been able to absorb the tensions and make something grow from them.

All have come to us. We are not the Great Southern Land. But strength should never be measured by size.

We are one of the world's youngest nations. We are the potiki and have the potiki's point of view.

Our strength is in our independence, our boldness, and in being sufficiently on the edge of things to be able to assess what is happening elsewhere. There may not be many of us, at just three and a half million people. But numbers do not matter either.

The Maori say that where there is one, there is a thousand.

We are the well at the bottom of the world.

Aotearoa New Zealand

Mt Tasman and Mt Cook, Southern Alps.

The Legendary Land

E tu te huru ma, haramai e noho, e tu te huru pango hanatu haere.

Let those with white hair sit, let those who are young and with black hair go out into the world.

Te Reinga to Auckland

The Maori name for the North Island is Te Ika a Maui, the fish of Maui. The fish, turned to stone by the sun's rays, has been lying here being eroded by the southern ocean for aeons. Considering this it's still in remarkable condition, looking rather like a giant manta ray sunning itself on the surface of the sea.

Maui's brothers made quite a meal of the fish, leaving their teeth marks across the landscape. The north, though, is the tail of the fish, where there's not much flesh. Ninety Mile Beach is a flick of stunning bleached bone sand, ending at Cape Reinga, the northernmost fin.

Te Reinga looks across Spirits Bay in the direction of the sun, and it is here that the Tasman and the Pacific Ocean meet. A lighthouse stands on the point and just below it is a place long revered by the Maori. At the end of our lives this is where we take leave of Aotearoa to return to the Hawaiki of our ancestors. We shed our tears of farewell before diving into the sea where the kelp opens to receive us.

Tradition has it that Northland is where Kupe, the Maori discoverer of Aotearoa, landed. When he took the news back to the legendary Hawaiki it was of a place of sunshine, beauty and incredible potential.

Today Northland remains the stuff that dreams are made of. The east coast is a complex of deep harbours with names that roll off the tongue like breakers coming in from the sea — Parengarenga, Houhora, Kerikeri — down to Whangarei, the main city of the north. The west coast is a maze of estuaries and shallow harbours, dominated by the Hokianga Harbour. Everywhere there are long sandy beaches and small sun-baked settlements snoozing in the sun. Once upon a time the rugged hills were totally covered with the kauri, King of Trees; although the majority were felled for the early shipbuilding industry there are still some stands remaining to remind us of the imposing forests that

The Legendary Land

touched the sky. Other places are haunted with memories of the kauri gumlands, where Maori and Dalmatian worked together.

You can tell why the Bay of Islands became the cradle of both Maori and Pakeha settlement; it has gentle slopes that trap the sun, and its myriad islands are like small fish bones spat out during an epic repast. However, its history is anything but gentle, which is why the Treaty of Waitangi between Maori and Pakeha came to be signed here in 1840.

From the grounds of the Treaty House you can look across to Paihia and Russell. Nearby Okiato was the site of New Zealand's first capital, but not for long. By 1841 a new capital had been found — Auckland.

Sprawled across the isthmus between the Manukau and Waitemata Harbours, Auckland has grown from a shantytown on the beach to become New Zealand's largest city, and the largest Polynesian city in the world. The Ngati Whatua are the main tribe. Their name for the city, Tamaki makau rau, is a tribute to the sexual prowess of a man by the name of Tamaki who was reputed to have a thousand lovers.

Today Auckland is in fact four cities — Auckland City itself, North Shore City, Manukau City and Waitakere City. The centrepiece of Auckland City is Queen Street, which runs up from the harbour to Karangahape Road, but throughout there are suburbs of distinctive charm and individuality. The dance clubs and restaurants of Ponsonby, Herne Bay, Parnell, Mission Bay and Devonport are always busy, while the Polynesian markets of South Auckland are vibrant and alive.

Auckland's natural configuration is complicated by volcanic cones, the most dramatic of which is Rangitoto Island. More than any other feature, Rangitoto is a physical icon for Aucklanders, symbolising their love of the outdoors and their wonderful harbour.

The revered Tane Mahuta, estimated to be 1,200 years old, is the most famous of all the kauri trees in the Waipoua Kauri Forest.

Te Reinga to Auckland

The sun comes up over Matauri Bay, Northland, awakening the legendary land.

The Legendary Land

Silver skies reflect in water made silver by the falling tide at Whangaroa Harbour. The fiordlike harbour, on the east coast of Northland, has one of the most dramatic entrances in New Zealand. The heads are dominated by the imposing features known as the domes of St Peter and St Paul. In 1809 Whangaroa Harbour was the scene of a massacre when sailors from the *Boyd*, sent ashore to cut spars of kauri, were killed. The *Boyd* was razed.

Te Reinga to Auckland

Hokianga Harbour, on the west coast, is a sinuous waterway into New Zealand history. Kupe is said to have departed from here to return to Hawaiki. As early as 1820 ships from the other side of the world were braving the surf to pick up kauri timber, and later, kauri gum. The Maori called the surf kaiwaka, or canoe eater.

Today the Hokianga is a place of sand dunes sculpted by wind and water.

The Legendary Land

Inland from the maze of sea rivers and mangroves, farmland takes over from the sea.

The Hokianga has become a place to escape to. You don't need much to live there, and yet you inherit Nature's bounty.

Te Reinga to Auckland

Situated on Kerikeri Inlet, Kerikeri was the second Anglican mission station in Aotearoa, built there so as to be close to the pa of the fighting chief Hongi Hika. Intact from those early days, the Stone Store is the oldest surviving stone building in New Zealand.

The Stone Store was built in 1832 as a storehouse for the mission, became an ammunition magazine during the 1840s, and today is a general store and museum.

The Legendary Land

The Treaty grounds, where the Treaty of Waitangi was signed in 1840, occupy a high promontory overlooking the sea. The Treaty House was sent out from Sydney to New Zealand in 1833, and became the home of James Busby, the British Resident.

On 6 February each year the grounds become a marae where thousands gather to commemorate the signing of the Treaty and to debate its meaning for Maori and Pakeha today.

Russell, originally known as Kororareka, was New Zealand's first European town, and Christ Church is New Zealand's oldest surviving church. The churchyard has the headstones of sailors from faraway Nantucket and Plymouth, and details of the first Pakeha to come to Aotearoa.

Te Reinga to Auckland

The imposing Maori meeting house on the Treaty Grounds at Waitangi was erected as a 1940 Centennial Memorial. Carved under the direction of the late Pine Taiapa, the meeting house is dedicated to the ideals of unity. Within are carvings in all the tribal styles of the Maori, incorporating all the famous ancestors of the people.

A Maori meeting house is always constructed to represent an ancestor. It has a head, backbone, ribcage and limbs. When you go into the house you enter into the ancestor or, if you like, you are taken into the body of the people.

The Legendary Land

Te Reinga to Auckland

A view of Russell, in the Bay of Islands. In its early days a place of sailors, ship deserters, runaways and thieves, its licentiousness was such that Charles Darwin called it 'the Hell-hole of the South Pacific'.

The Legendary Land

Despite Russell's undesirable reputation, the French Bishop Pompallier in 1839 decided to move his Roman Catholic mission here from the Hokianga. The town was subsequently sacked by Maori in 1845 but Pompallier House was one of those that survived.

Bishop Pompallier himself never lived in the house, which stands on Russell's waterfront. It is now a museum illustrating the early days of Russell and the French mission.

Te Reinga to Auckland

The sundial on Flagstaff Hill, overlooking Russell and the superb Bay of Islands. During the first years of New Zealand's nationhood, the hill was where the British flag used to fly, only to be repeatedly chopped down by the Ngapuhi chief Hone Heke; once in 1844 and three times in 1845. Although Heke had earlier signed the Treaty of Waitangi, the flag became a hated symbol of the way the land had passed to Queen Victoria.

The Legendary Land

New Zealand is a country of waterfalls, reminders of the water which rushed away from Maui's fish as it broached the surface of the sea. These are the Whangarei Falls, east of Northland's main city, Whangarei, on the road to Ngunguru.

Te Reinga to Auckland

Auckland by night is a kaleidoscope of lights and entertainment. The City of Sails lights up across the water at evening, the highrise buildings like sails in the darkness. Below, small boats are at anchorage.

The Legendary Land

The Aotea Centre has weathered local controversy — people either love it or hate it — to become Auckland city's main venue for international conferences and festivals, musicals, opera and orchestral concerts. The gateway to the Centre is the work of Maori artist Selwyn Muru.

Te Reinga to Auckland

A modern day Maui, a window washer scales the daunting heights of Auckland's high-tech cityscape.

The Legendary Land

Auckland Museum, in the Domain, has one of the best views of Auckland City and the harbour. The museum features major exhibitions of Maori and Polynesian artefacts and regularly hosts Maori cultural performances in its great Maori court, dominated by Hotunui, the carved meeting house, and a magnificent war canoe, *Te Toki a Tapiri*. During the summer, the Domain hosts free opera and orchestral performances in the park, attracting over 150,000 people to nights of song, music, laser and firework displays.

Te Reinga to Auckland

The Legendary Land

Auckland attracts musicians of all types who perform on the busy streets or in the city's bars and cafes.

The Topp Twins are a national institution. A singing duo, they really are twins.

Te Reinga to Auckland

The Legendary Land

One Tree Hill is one of the many volcanic cones that dot the Auckland landscape. It rivals Rangitoto for the title of Auckland's most well known physical feature. Once a palisaded Maori pa, it is a favourite lookout spot. It is still a hill of one tree, the second on the site, as the first was felled by an early colonist. Nearby stands an obelisk built in honour of the Maori people.

Te Reinga to Auckland

Fireworks and dragons bring a touch of Asia to a Polynesian city at Auckland's Oriental Markets.

The Legendary Land

The Civic Theatre is one of the wonders of the cinema world. An Art Deco movie palace of the 1920s, it is a Xanadu, a lush Babylonian temple to fantasy. Stars twinkle in a midnight blue dome, surrounded by extravagant friezes and sculptures.

Te Reinga to Auckland

The Legendary Land

Auckland, City of Sails, where marinas dot the bays. At Westhaven Marina, yachts from all over the world jostle and sway beneath the cliffs of St Mary's Bay and in sight of the Auckland Harbour Bridge.

Waikato to the Volcanic Plateau

When the first Polynesians arrived they brought the mauri or life-giving forces which would make the land blossom. Until this time the land was profane, without sacredness.

The ancestors of the Maori often spent years sailing the coast, when appropriate blessing the land with the sacred gifts of the ancient hearth of Hawaiki: the prayers, incantations and seeds of knowledge that would enable Aotearoa to become the legendary land.

Most of the canoe voyagers made landfall on the east coast. But two canoes, the fabled *Tainui* and the *Tokomaru*, did it the hard way, travelling around the top of the island and down the less hospitable west coast. Halfway down the coast, the *Tainui* came across three imposing harbours, Raglan, Aotea, and Kawhia, where it finally came to rest; the *Tokomaru* travelled south as far as the Mokau River.

The Ngati Maniapoto live here in what became known as the King Country. During the Land Wars of the 1860s the Maori King Tawhiao threw his hat on a map of New Zealand and said, 'Where the hat lands I will protect all those who have given offence to the Queen of England.' The hat landed on the King Country.

The stronghold of the Maori Kings is in the Waikato. It is the Turangawaewae marae at Ngaruawahia, a proud complex of buildings which was begun by Princess Te Puea in the 1920s. Not far away is Taupiri Mountain,

The Legendary Land

where the Maori Kings are buried. Through this mystical landscape winds the mighty Waikato River, reputed to have a taniwha or river monster at every bend. Each year in March war canoes sail on the river as part of an annual celebration of Kingitanga, the heritage of the Maori King movement.

Because of its closeness to Auckland, the Waikato was a natural destination for Pakeha. Missionaries came first, setting up a mission station at Mangapouri. Then came the settlers, pouring down the military road and over the lip of the Bombay Hills. The great Waikato River, the Mississippi of New Zealand, enabled access to the more impenetrable corners of the plains.

Right at the heart of the North Island is the Volcanic Plateau. This is an area of thermal vulcanism which actually runs from White Island on the east coast diagonally through Rotorua down to Taupo and the mountains of Tongariro National Park. It is one of New Zealand's most awe-inspiring areas.

At Whakarewarewa Village, in Rotorua, Maori culture forms part of a theatrical backdrop of mudpools, hot springs, drifting steam and spouting geysers. Whakarewarewa, however, is just one of the many thermal areas of the volcanic plateau. If you want to be reminded of a more ferocious aspect of the area visit Waiotapu or the Waimangu Valley. In this region, in 1886, Mount Tarawera erupted, destroying the fabulous Pink and White Terraces. Drive on to Taupo, and when you swim in the lake, go yachting or fish for trout, just remember that once upon a time this was a volcano that blew its top.

Modern science has its own logical explanation of these geothermal phenomena, reminding us that New Zealand is on the volcanic 'Rim of Fire'. The Maori version, however, is different.

The High Priest Ngatoroirangi arrived on the *Arawa* canoe. During his travels inland he saw Tongariro Mountain sparkling in the distance. He had never seen snow before so he climbed the mountain, accompanied by his manservant, Ngauruhoe. As the cold began to claim them Ngatoroirangi chanted to his priestess sisters in far off Hawaiki, on the other side of the sun. The sisters invoked a sacred flame and sent it rushing beneath the Pacific Ocean and down to New Zealand. The fire first surfaced at White Island, then burst out in the centre of the North Island. Wherever it surfaced it created hot springs, geysers and volcanic mountains — Rotorua, Taupo, Waiotapu, Orakei Korako, Wairakei, Turangi, and the triad mountains of Tongariro, Ngauruhoe and Ruapehu.

And what of Ngatoroirangi and Ngauruhoe, you ask? The sacred flame came just in time to save the High Priest but, aue, it was too late for Ngauruhoe, who perished, giving his name to a mountain.

Waikato to the Volcanic Plateau

The mysterious Waikato River, revered by the Maori, is the longest in Aotearoa. As Maui's fish loomed out of the sea, the water began runnelling from the Waikato's source in the snow-capped mountains of the Volcanic Plateau into the basin now known as Lake Taupo. From there it found a trench eaten by Maui's brothers through steep uplands to the Hamilton plains. It swept through Taupiri Gorge and found the sea at Port Waikato.

The Legendary Land

Light glistens on the sea at the mouth of the Marokopa River, south of Kawhia Harbour.

Waikato to the Volcanic Plateau

The Legendary Land

'Kia hiwa ra! Kia hiwa ra!' Be alert! Be watchful! A Maori sentinel, bold against a crimsoning sky, stands to welcome visitors in the Ohaki Maori village on the approach to the Waitomo Caves.

The caves, carved out of the limestone by underground streams, are home to millions of tiny glow-worms. For the adventurous, a black-water rafting tour provides a thrilling introduction to one of the world's natural wonders.

Waikato to the Volcanic Plateau

The Legendary Land

On 31 May 1886 a ghostly war canoe was seen skimming across the surface of Lake Tarawera. Those on board had their heads bowed and wore the feathers of death in their hair. The sighting was taken as an omen of disaster. Eleven days later, on 10 June 1886, Mount Tarawera exploded. The fabulous Pink and White Terraces were destroyed. Three Maori villages were obliterated. 153 people were killed.

Today the colossal forces of the eruption have left a huge crack across the land. Forest has regenerated on the lower slopes of the crater.

Waikato to the Volcanic Plateau

Rotorua's most famous Maori attraction is Whakarewarewa Reserve, but others also vie for attention. Te Takinga marae, for instance, boasts a striking brilliant red meeting house whose bargeboards cut like an arrow against the blue of the sky. The figure at the top is a Maori warrior holding a taiaha in the posture of challenge. The whole meeting house is intricately carved and woven.

There are a number of stories of how carving came to the Maori. One of them tells of a brave father, Rua, whose son was taken by the sea people to an underwater meeting house. Rua fought the sea people, or ponaturi, and on his return to the surface of the water brought back the carved slabs of that underwater building. These aquatic treasures became the basis for carving design.

The Legendary Land

One of the highlights of the Whakarewarewa Reserve is the Pohutu Geyser, which shoots steam to over 18 metres. In an area only 1 km long and 500 metres wide, more than 500 hot springs bubble and spurt.

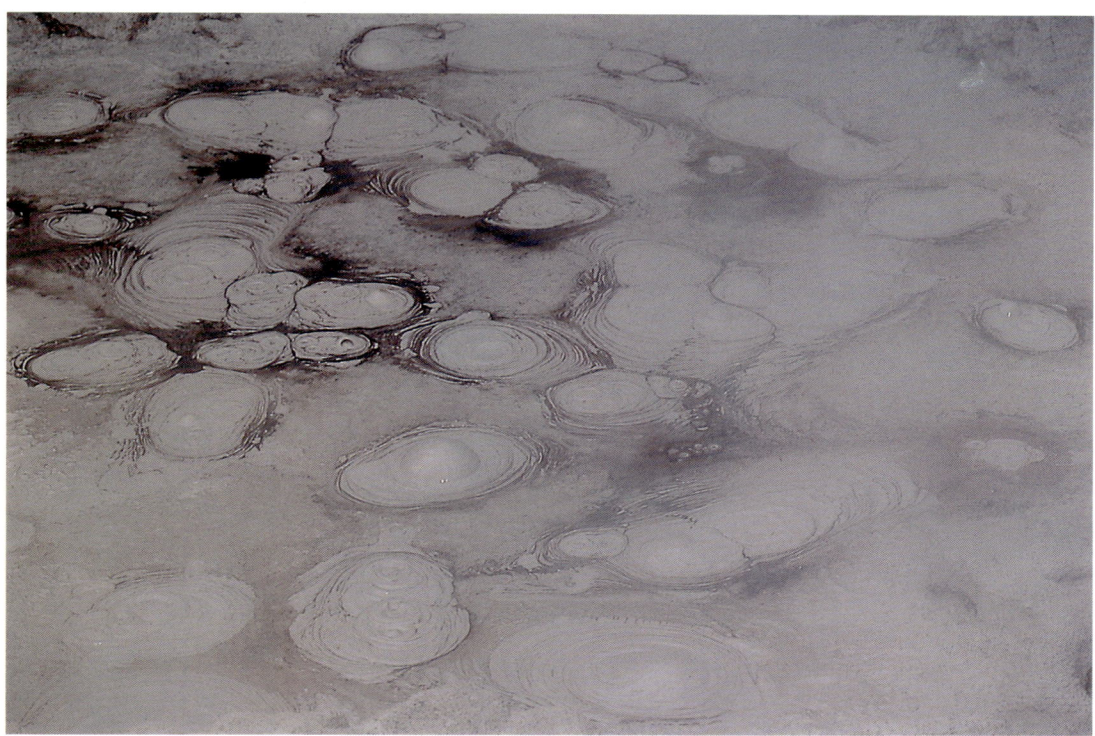

Waikato to the Volcanic Plateau

Visitors come to Whakarewarewa not only to look at the mudpools and geysers but also to experience Maori culture and to witness Maori craftsmen at work. Whakarewarewa has become an important school of learning for Maori craftsmen and women. Their art includes finely crafted handweapons, personal jewellery, statuettes, woven mats and baskets.

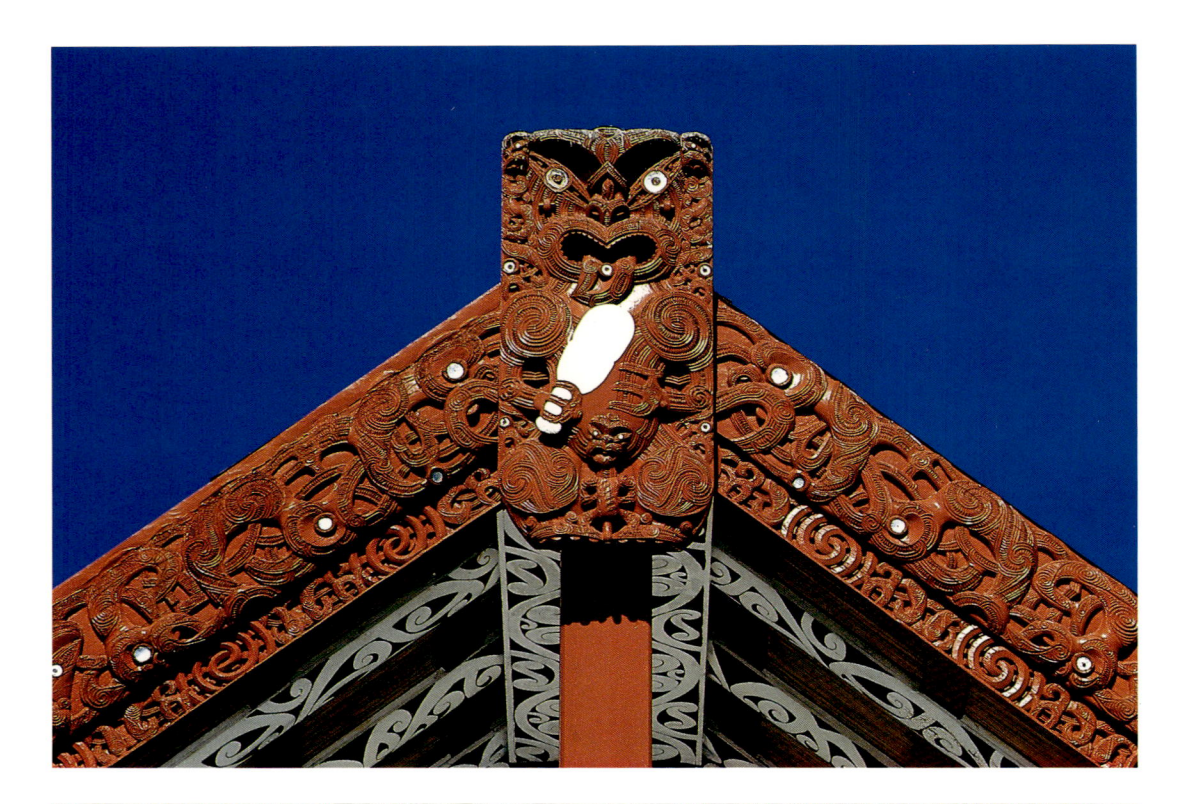

60

The Legendary Land

'Tena koe.' Greetings are exchanged at Whakarewarewa. The secret of the hongi, the Maori greeting, is not to rub noses but to press them together gently.

61

Waikato to the Volcanic Plateau

The Legendary Land

Midway between Rotorua and Taupo is the Waiotapu Scenic Reserve, whose name means 'sacred waters'. One of its chief attractions is the Champagne Pool, with colours ranging from red-ochre to acidic yellow.

Further south is the Wairakei thermal area.

Waikato to the Volcanic Plateau

Flax grows beside the Waikato River as it flows from Lake Taupo on its journey to the sea.

The Legendary Land

Lake Taupo and the surrounding waterways offer exhilarating fishing to visiting anglers. The brightly lit emblem celebrates the lure of the trout.

Waikato to the Volcanic Plateau

Mt Tongariro and Mt Ngauruhoe, Tongariro National Park.

The Legendary Land

Kia mau koe ki te kupu a tou matua.

Hold fast to the words that your father gives you.

Waikato to the Volcanic Plateau

In 1887 the Maori chief Te Heuheu Tukino gifted the peaks of the Tongariro mountains to the New Zealand Government, creating the basis of New Zealand's first national park.

Now covering more than 79,000 hectares, the Park is dominated by three active volcanoes. Ruapehu, the tallest at 2,797 metres, is the highest mountain in the North Island. At its summit is a steaming crater lake.

The Legendary Land

Numerous walking tracks in the Tongariro National Park take you through a range of bush and alpine terrains. The waterfalls of the area are spectacular additions to a landscape of unparalleled diversity.

Coromandel to the Wairarapa

It was at Mercury Bay, on the Coromandel Peninsula, that James Cook raised the flag of Britain and claimed the area for George III, in November 1769. He also observed the transit of Mercury over the South Pacific, hence the name of the bay.

In those days the Coromandel provided an impenetrable screen of lush fern and kauri forest. Like the Northland forests, however, the kauri of Coromandel were soon felled for the ship-building industry. Gold was discovered at Thames and Waihi in 1867, and the gold industry flourished until early this century.

Today gold is once again being mined at Waihi, but Coromandel is better known for the golden sand of its beaches and the wild beauty of its peninsula. When rain curtains the awesome cliffs, when the lush bush becomes a fall of glistening green cascading into the blue of the sea, you can almost imagine a canoe chant rising over the horizon:

Toia mai, te waka! Ki te urunga, te waka!
Paddle the canoe! Bring it to its berth!
To its sleeping place! To the place of its landing!

The place of landing, for most of the great Maori canoes, was the Bay of Plenty. The *Tainui*, *Te Arawa* and *Mataatua* all landed here; the *Takitimu* paused but then sailed onward, for its destiny lay further south. As a result the Maori presence here is an imposing one. When Pakeha settled the area, it was developed into sheep and cattle country, but today oranges, kiwifruit and grapes have taken over. Way out on the skyline volcanic White Island still occasionally drifts plumes of smoke to the horizon.

South of the Bay of Plenty is East Cape. This is where you find Mount Hikurangi, that part of Maui's fish which reared up just beneath his canoe and

The Legendary Land

caught it within a fold of skin. Hikurangi is the sacred mountain of the Ngati Porou, the people who live around the Cape.

Inland from the Cape are the mysterious Ureweras, home of the Tuhoe people. They are descended not from any canoe but from the marriage of mist with mountain. From this people came the brilliant military campaigner and founder of the Ringatu church, Te Kooti Arikirangi, and the charismatic leader Rua Kenana. Their kingdom is a mountain fortress guarded by rocky terrain, silver waterfalls and lakes.

They are the Children of the Mist.

On the southern side of the Cape is Poverty Bay, where James Cook made landing on 9 October 1769. The white cliffs just outside Gisborne, the main city of the Cape, are named Young Nick's Head, after his ship's boy.

Protected by rugged hills on three sides and the sea to the east, Gisborne has grown in a special way. People seem a lot more genuine here and they walk more slowly. Once there was just one set of traffic lights. Now there are four.

The beaches around the Cape, Poverty Bay and down through Hawke's Bay are among the most magnificent in New Zealand, and the whole coast resonates with history, both Maori and Pakeha.

The main tribe of Hawke's Bay is the Kahungunu, who take their name from an incredibly virile ancestor who was the Don Juan of Maoridom. His physical attributes were such, it is said, that at the sight of him both women and men went weak at the knees.

Hawke's Bay is the home of some of New Zealand's great sheep stations. More recently its Mediterranean climate has encouraged its people to diversify into horticulture, market gardening and orcharding. Half of New Zealand's wine is made in Hawke's Bay. The twin cities of the area, Napier and Hastings, were severely damaged in an earthquake in 1931. Napier was reconstructed in the angular, jazzy, Art Deco style and today is known as the Art Deco Capital of the World.

Then there's the Wairarapa, one of the first regions in New Zealand to be settled by Europeans. The country's first sheep station was established here in 1844. Today the area's agricultural heritage is highlighted when the main city of the Wairarapa, Masterton, hosts the annual Golden Shears competition. Nearby Martinborough is consolidating its reputation as a producer of top quality wines, forming part of a relatively new industry that is of growing significance to New Zealand.

Coromandel to the Wairarapa

Tairua Harbour, Coromandel Peninsula.

The Legendary Land

**He pai kanohi, he maene kiri, he ra te kai ma tono poho,
   Waihoki, he pai kupu kau.**

**A beautiful face, a soft skin, a breast kissed by the sun,
   Such is an idle promise.**

Coromandel to the Wairarapa

The Legendary Land

'Ki te whai ao, ki te ao marama!' 'It is coming, the world of light!' The east coast of the Coromandel Peninsula looks straight across the ocean to the place where the sun rises. Dawn brings colours ranging from the most delicate ochres and pinks to cerise, violet and vermillion.

Here at Opoutere, the first fingers of light touch boats at anchor and the estuary.

Coromandel to the Wairarapa

The eastern side of Coromandel Peninsula offers an everchanging vista of golden sands, bush-clad slopes and unusual rock formations, such as here at Cathedral Cove.

The Legendary Land

Sheep graze quietly in paddocks near Hahei, overlooking the sea.

Wherever you go in New Zealand you will always find sheep. They are 'the golden fleece', successfully introduced to New Zealand in 1834. Today sheepfarming is still one of the cornerstones of the New Zealand economy.

Coromandel to the Wairarapa

Driving Creek, the creation of potter Barry Brickell, is both a working environment for artists and the setting for a miniature railway that takes visitors up through the bush to a view across the Coromandel Peninsula.

78

The Legendary Land

Coromandel to the Wairarapa

Young schoolchildren at Ruatoki School work hard and play hard, preparing for the future of Aotearoa.

'E tipu e rea ...' 'Grow up, young and tender plant, grasping the tools of the Pakeha in one hand, the treasures of your ancestors in the other, looking to God to whom all things belong.'

Sir Apirana Ngata, a distinguished Parliamentarian of the first part of this century, wrote these words in the book of a young Maori schoolchild. The words are as relevant today as they ever were. Regardless of culture or country, children are the greatest taonga, or treasures, in the world.

The Legendary Land

Coromandel to the Wairarapa

White Island, Bay of Plenty.

The Legendary Land

Tama tu tama ora, tama noho tama mate.

If you stand you live, if you lie down you die.

Coromandel to the Wairarapa

It is told that after Maui had fished up the land he took a step onto the North Island. His feet caught up some of the fire that was burning on it. As he shook off the fire, it fell into the sea, creating the island known as Whakaari to the Maori but renamed White Island by Captain Cook.

Sulphur was mined on the island intermittently between 1885 and 1936, and the remains of old mining equipment can still be found.

The Legendary Land

From the Bay of Plenty there are two roads to Gisborne. The fast way takes you through the splendid Waioeka Gorge. The slow way, around the spectacular Coast, takes you along seemingly endless stretches of farmland and beach.

85

Coromandel to the Wairarapa

The East Coast waters are famous for their succulent shellfish, or kai moana. Delicacies include paua and crayfish, here being prepared for a local celebration.

The Legendary Land

Produce from the land is valued as highly as that from the sea. Since the arrival of the Pakeha, sheep, pig and cattle farming have become a significant part of life on the Coast.

87

Coromandel to the Wairarapa

Hui, or gatherings, are one of the great joys of Maori life. Whether birthday, wedding or funeral, they are always open occasions when Maori celebrate the values of aroha (love), whanaungatanga (family) and manaakitanga (togetherness). The meeting house and marae are the venue for the hui. Out the back a hangi, or earth oven, is put down by the men to feed the visitors.

The Legendary Land

Coromandel to the Wairarapa

The Legendary Land

Cape Kidnappers, called Te Matau a Maui by the Maori, is said to be what remained of Maui's hook after he had fished up New Zealand. If so, judging by the jagged headland, the hook must have had pretty wicked barbs.

A short drive from the city of Napier, Cape Kidnappers is now more well known as a gannet colony. Male gannets start arriving around mid-July and are joined by their life-long mates soon after. Chicks hatch in the later part of the year, making November and December the best times to visit the colony.

Coromandel to the Wairarapa

Sunrise casts a soft glow over the Art Deco fountain on Napier's waterfront.

The Legendary Land

Typical of coast vistas in the Wairarapa are those at Castlepoint, some 68 km east of Masterton, the main centre of the Wairarapa.

93

Coromandel to the Wairarapa

The Legendary Land

Castlepoint lighthouse stands like a sentinel above a tiny fishing and holiday settlement.

In earlier times this was where Kupe, the legendary discoverer of Aotearoa, began an epic voyage in pursuit of an enormous wheke, or octopus, which had stolen the bait from his line.

Taranaki to Wellington

The story of Taranaki (also known as Mt Egmont) is of a lover who once lived with the other male mountains Tongariro, Ruapehu, Putuaki and Tauhara in the centre of the North Island. All were in love with Pihanga, a female mountain, and fought great battles to win her heart. They hurled rocks, lava and belching gases at one another, and filled the air with dark clouds. In the end it was Tongariro who won, and the defeated mountains, Taranaki among them, were banished. Taranaki moved west, his weight chiselling out the riverbed of the Whanganui River.

On a clear day, Taranaki can be seen from the South Island. It made itself known to the earliest Maori canoe voyagers but when Abel Tasman sailed past in 1642 it hid itself from him. However, for James Cook in 1770 Taranaki was kinder. He saw it through cloud and rain, with lightning dancing around its crown. In 1841 ships of the New Zealand Company arrived from England's Plymouth and, within the gaze of Taranaki, established the settlement of New Plymouth.

As elsewhere in New Zealand, Taranaki's history bears the marks of conflict between settlers and Maori. Parihaka Pa was the centre of a remarkable episode of Maori passive resistance — the pa was razed to the ground in 1881.

To the south of Taranaki graceful Wanganui city is a centre for exploration of the Whanganui river valley. The beauty of the river valleys is a taonga, a treasure, a tipuna or ancestral right, for all the coming generations.

Today, the Whanganui's deep gorges, waterfalls and wilderness have a special attraction for those who would explore it by canoe, white-river raft or jetboat. The Rangitikei and Manawatu rivers, further inland, are just as stunning. The Manawatu was created by a giant totara tree which was set in motion by the gods. Crashing its way from Hawke's Bay, across the mountains, it carved out the Manawatu Gorge before reaching the Tasman Sea. At the seaward end

The Legendary Land

of the gorge is the largest city of the plains, Palmerston North, a major centre for research and education.

Maui's brothers made a good meal of the land further to the south, leaving the terrain pretty flat all the way to Wellington.

The lowland is dressed with strands of sand dune country drained by swamp and stream. Some bony ridges are left where the forests were felled and replaced with grassland. Once sheep country, the Horowhenua — and the Golden Coast — now has a thriving horticultural and market gardening industry. Offshore, Kapiti Island dominates the seascape. The great Ngati Toa chief, Te Rauparaha, used Kapiti as his island fortress in the 1820s. Today it is a bird sanctuary.

Some people find similarities between Wellington, which succeeded Auckland as the capital of New Zealand, and San Francisco. The colourful wooden houses of Oriental Parade edge a harbour which must surely be one of the most splendid in the world. A busy port, Wellington is the terminal for traffic across Cook Strait, linking the North Island with the South Island.

The Maori history of Wellington is associated with three Maori discoverers, the legendary Kupe and the two sons of Whatonga — Tara and Tautoki — around AD 1100. Some still call Wellington by its Maori name, Te Whanganui-a-Tara, The Great Harbour of Tara.

Today Wellington is one of New Zealand's most cultured and vibrant cities. The suburbs of Wellington all retain their own special character. Newtown, for example, is a mix of Maori, Pacific Island, Greek and new immigrant families, creating a joyful blend of fun and excitement. In recent years the waterfront and inner city have been transformed into a showcase of art, music, theatre and culture similar to Vancouver, Toronto and Sydney. Every second year Wellington hosts a magnificent International Festival of the Arts, and an accompanying Fringe Festival.

Wellington was the home of New Zealand's most famous short story writer, Katherine Mansfield (1888–1923). The central city, with its distinctive 'Beehive', would be unrecognisable to Mansfield today, but there is still something of the quality she describes in her stories in the older parts of the city — around Old Saint Paul's, Mount Victoria or Tinakori Road.

Taranaki to Wellington

Taranaki is New Zealand's most climbed mountain and the jewel of Egmont National Park. The mountain casts its mana, or prestige, over the whole province. Chiefs and revered ancestors are buried here, close to the sky.

The Legendary Land

Constant eruptions have sculpted the present shape of Mount Taranaki. The dark-forested lower slopes contrast with the softer colours of the Taranaki farmland.

Taranaki to Wellington

The Whanganui River, the second longest in the North Island, flows west from Mount Tongariro to Taumarunui then turns south to sweep over rapids and through narrow gorges to the sea.

The river has always been a major area of Maori settlement, and with the coming of the Pakeha, mission stations were established on the river, each bearing a Biblical name. The great New Zealand poet, James K. Baxter, spent his final years at Hiruharama or Jerusalem.

The Legendary Land

Whanganui National Park, which encompasses 79,000 hectares of lowland forest on both sides of the river, was opened in 1987.

Today, the Whanganui is popular with canoeists, trampers and others seeking adventure. Ramanui Lodge, a restored pioneer homestead, provides a last touch of comfort before they head for the isolation of the bush-clad hills.

Taranaki to Wellington

Light falls softly on Oriental Bay in Wellington, capital city of New Zealand.

The Legendary Land

Taranaki to Wellington

The city of Wellington lies enclosed within hills, harbour and sky. Just below the vantage point of Tinakori Hill lies the old suburb of Thorndon, with the modern city centre beyond.

The Legendary Land

A familiar Wellington landmark, the Cable Car links the heart of the business centre with the University suburb of Kelburn.

Taranaki to Wellington

The Legendary Land

Inner city development under a progressive city administration has transformed the look of Wellington and turned it into an exciting international cultural and conference destination. The architecture is innovative, as seen in the crown of this skyscraper building, looking rather like a minimalist version of the Statue of Liberty.

Wellingtonians are particularly proud of their Civic Square, with its paved courtyard and tiled fountains. The metallic nikau palm is part of a colonnade that borders a modern library building.

Taranaki to Wellington

The Legendary Land

Wellington at sunset, viewed from Mt Victoria.

Nelson and Marlborough to Kaikoura

According to a Ngai Tahu story of the creation of Aotearoa, the South Island is Te Waka o Aoraki, the canoe belonging to Aoraki. This was a canoe, not of men but of gods, which struck an underwater reef and was wrecked. As the water began to flood the canoe, Aoraki and his brother gods climbed higher and higher to escape drowning. The sun came up and, as with Maui's fish, they all turned to stone. So the Southern Alps came into being. Of all the mountains Aoraki, or Mount Cook, is the highest. The heights of the other mountains reflect their seniority.

If you look at the South Island it is not too difficult to imagine it as a petrified canoe tilted into the sea. The Marlborough Sounds are the remains of its intricately carved prow. Bluff Hill, way down south, is the stern. Clinging to one side are the Southern Alps, Aoraki and his brothers. The rest of the canoe is strewn with the remains of its cargo in the form of lower mountain ranges and hillocks. Stewart Island is the anchor.

According to Maori tradition the great lakes of the South Island were not created by glaciers either. A voyager from another canoe, the *Uruao*, was responsible. His name was Rakaihaitu, and wherever he scratched the surface of the land with his digging stick a lake was formed.

Today many travellers get their first glimpse of the South Island from the Cook Strait ferry as it enters the Marlborough Sounds. Most do not realise that they are sailing through the half-sunken prow of Aoraki's wrecked canoe.

The Legendary Land

The Sounds are magical sea-filled valleys which provide spectacular sailing and swimming. Their shores are clothed with unspoilt bush. Some of the islands further out are home to New Zealand's tuatara, a living link back to the dinosaurs of old.

Inland from the Sounds, the perspective changes. High tussock and alpine country overlook gentle river valleys and the sprawling Wairau Plains. Marlborough was once the home of great sheep stations, but today orchards, vineyards and berry fields dominate the landscape. The soil, and the sun, are particularly conducive to fine wine production and as a result Marlborough is home to some of New Zealand's best, and biggest, wineries.

West of Marlborough is Nelson, described by Abel Tasman in 1642 as 'a great land uplifted high'. Nelson shares with Blenheim one of the best climates in the country. Its beaches are golden sand swept by sparkling sea, the townships are colourful and friendly, and fruit trees, vines and berries flourish amid valleys of trees and ferns.

Nelson City, established by the New Zealand Company in 1842, is the centre of the province. Today it is a delightful mix of modernity and old world charm. Although its traditional industry remains horticulture, the area's rich fishing grounds have now turned Nelson into the biggest fishing port in New Zealand. The city is also a magnet for artisans — jewellers, potters, glassworkers and sculptors — who create some of New Zealand's finest craftworks. Close by is Abel Tasman National Park, a wonderful area of golden beaches, steep granite formations, limestone caves and native forest.

Nelson is renowned for its glorious beaches. Magnificent Tahunanui is only a short walk from the centre of Nelson city.

The Kaikoura coast follows the Pacific seaboard all the way down to Canterbury. Whaling was once a major industry along the coast. Today, the more gentle art of whalewatching provides an opportunity to witness some of the world's most beautiful creatures.

Driving south, the spectacular Kaikoura Ranges lie to the west and the indomitable sea to the east. The coast is one of many moods — ever-shifting cloudscapes vie with swirling giant kelp to create moko, or tattoos, across the land. And always, there are the mountains.

Nelson and Marlborough to Kaikoura

The shattered prow of the Marlborough Sounds comprises two main inlets, a maze of channels and myriad islands, all within a heavily wooded and mountainous landscape. Protected from the wind and currents, the sea often becomes transformed into surfaces that are as smooth as glass. Much of the Sounds can only be reached by boat, but there are a few roads, providing a route for both people and livestock.

The Legendary Land

Sunset over Titirangi Bay draws the curtain on one of New Zealand's most fascinating landscapes, the interlocking labyrinths of sea valleys and ridges known as the Marlborough Sounds.

Nelson and Marlborough to Kaikoura

A mural of Aotearoa painted on a blank concrete wall in Wakefield Quay, Nelson.

The Legendary Land

Nelson and Marlborough to Kaikoura

Etched sand at Awaroa Inlet, Abel Tasman National Park.

The Legendary Land

Ka pu te ruha, ka hao te rangatahi.

The worn-out net is cast aside, the new net goes fishing.

Nelson and Marlborough to Kaikoura

Sunlight streaming through ferns makes a fascinating study of light and shade in the forest of Abel Tasman National Park.

At 22,500 hectares the Park is New Zealand's smallest, but it is one of the most beautiful.

The Legendary Land

The Park is noted for its wonderful coastline, and its long summers attract holidaymakers who explore its caves, lagoons, and strands of golden sand. Inland, broken granite and limestone country draws trampers and cavers.

Nelson and Marlborough to Kaikoura

Morning mist, Kaikoura.

The Legendary Land

He wahine, he whenua, e ngaro ai te tangata.

It is always over women and land that men fight.

121

Nelson and Marlborough to Kaikoura

There have been Maori settlements on the Kaikoura Peninsula from earliest times. The local Maori have a proud history of defending their turangawaewae (place to stand) and with good reason — the sea's bounty is a rich legacy.

The Legendary Land

Kaikoura's fame has been based on its harvests of crayfish, and indeed the name Kaikoura means 'a feed of crays'. As with the best things, however, they always seem to be in the most difficult places. You have to be skilful to harvest the sea.

Nelson and Marlborough to Kaikoura

The Legendary Land

What better way to see the Kaikouras than to sail off one of their high hills and paraglide in the strong currents which lift above the Peninsula.

Whalewatching, from a little nearer the ground, is one of the main reasons for visiting Kaikoura today. To the Maori, whales were rangatira or chieftains of the sea. The sperm whale, because of its strength and its formidable teeth, was especially highly regarded. Many great chiefs were likened to the sperm whale, and would often wear whale-tooth necklaces as a sign of strength.

Christchurch and Canterbury

There is another Ngai Tahu story, about a canoe called the *Araiteuru*, which must have come sailing down the east coast of the South Island after it had been formed. Incredible transformations occurred to those voyagers also. When some dived overboard and swam ashore they became mountains — among them, Mount Grey in Marlborough, Mount Tapuaenuku in the Kaikouras, Mount Torlesse near Christchurch, and Mount Somers near Ashburton. A fierce storm drove *Araiteuru* onward to Shag Point where it was wrecked; both the canoe and its captain were turned into a reef. The cargo of eelpots, calabashes and food became the famous Moeraki boulders. The three great waves and cross-wave which sank the canoe were turned into mountain ranges.

The remaining crew managed to swim ashore, and as it was cold they began to look for firewood. One of the women, Puketapu, went as far as the Clutha River, but on the way back she dropped some of her sticks — these became forests. At Palmerston, the coming of sunlight transformed Puketapu into a hill.

Another canoe voyager, Aonui, was turned into a slender rock pillar as he returned from collecting water from the Mataura River. A third voyager suffered a similar fate, turned by the sunlight into a hill of red ochre at Kaitangata.

Altogether, it is said, over 150 mountains and ranges in the South Island are people who were turned to stone.

Today these mountains of the South Island dominate the landscape. They are sentinels of the southern sky, with passes like narrow gateways through to the West Coast. For the traveller they provide an everchanging vista of immense power and beauty. For skiers, the mountains are Shangri La indeed. New Zealand's longest glacier, the Tasman, is located in Mt Cook National Park. Skiplanes regularly set down skiers at the top of the glacier for a fabulous run down a magical river of ice and snow.

The Legendary Land

For the rest, the immense Canterbury Plains, once the home of the giant moa, seem to roll on forever. The Ngai Tahu tribe were the first to live in this country of golden grass. From the air, the plains look like a vast pastoral ocean of patchwork green and gold, interrupted every now and then by the blue-grey of an intricately braided river.

In 1840 the French established a settlement at Akaroa, on Banks Peninsula, a township which today still maintains a piquant Gallic flavour. But it wasn't until 1848 and the establishment of the Canterbury Association in London that the idea of founding an Anglican settlement in New Zealand was formulated. Two years later, in 1850, four ships — the *Randolph*, *Charlotte Jane*, *Cressy* and *Sir George Seymour* — landed at Lyttelton. The idea was to transplant a model English society, complete with a bishop, gentry, tradespeople and other workers, people known for their respectability and high morals. The result was a South Seas version of Britain that has no parallel in New Zealand.

Nowhere is this more apparent than in Christchurch, the largest city of the South Island. The sheep-farming industry upon which Canterbury's prosperity is based enabled the gentry to build a thoroughly English city. The cathedral triumphs in the centre, and church spires spike the sky. Amid drifting willows the river Avon wends its way through a city of Gothic architecture and ever-changing colours. The green banks and parks blossom with flowers in spring, transforming the city into a colourful garden. Walk around the old university buildings, now transformed into an Arts Centre, or visit some of the city's older schools, splendid amid leafy settings, and you would think you were in an English university town.

Sheep graze on winter pasture beside Lake Tekapo, South Canterbury.

There is, of course, also a 'new' Christchurch, vibrant and ambitious, which reminds you quite firmly that the city is looking very much to the future. A busy airport, a growing reputation as an industrial city utilising the best of modern technology, and progressive city planning have made Christchurch one of the most positive of New Zealand's cities.

Christchurch and Canterbury

Arthur's Pass, on the main divide of the Southern Alps, is the gateway between Westland and North Canterbury. The Pass is part of Arthur's Pass National Park, which boasts magnificent chains of mountains and peaks, and wonderful beech forests. Below the Pass valleys enclose the braided rivers so typical of the Canterbury landscape.

The Legendary Land

This is the kind of panoramic vista that inspires people like artist Alec Cormack to capture North Canterbury's special beauty on canvas.

Christchurch and Canterbury

The road between Arthur's Pass and Christchurch winds through striking hill country. These rock outcrops are near Porter Heights, one of the area's popular skifields.

The Legendary Land

The hills finally meet the plains near the small town of Springfield. The huge haybales that are harvested in summer will help the high country stock through the harsh winter months.

Christchurch and Canterbury

In this city of contrasts both tradition and the necessary breaking of tradition are celebrated.

In 1893 the women of New Zealand were the first to exercise their right to vote in a national election. One of the leaders of the campaign for women's suffrage was Christchurch's Kate Sheppard.

Tradition is strongly upheld at Christ's College. The school was founded soon after the city itself, and is based on the model of an English public school.

132

The Legendary Land

Christchurch is a city of parks, meandering rivers — and wizards. Well, just one wizard, who can usually be found haranguing a willing crowd in Cathedral Square.

Christchurch and Canterbury

The Legendary Land

Christchurch glitters like a necklace strewn carelessly over the plains, as the sun sets and the moon appears over the city.

Christchurch and Canterbury

The Legendary Land

A view over Akaroa Harbour. With a longer Maori and European history than the rest of Canterbury, Banks Peninsula is of great archaeological interest. Pa sites and relics of the early trading days abound.

Christchurch and Canterbury

The Church of the Good Shepherd, on the shores of Lake Tekapo, was built to acknowledge the sacrifices of the early runholders, who braved hardship, freezing winters and blizzards to open up the surrounding Mackenzie Country.

The Legendary Land

139

Christchurch and Canterbury

The Legendary Land

To the east of Lake Tekapo lies the Two Thumb Range, gently dusted with snow in this winter landscape.

Christchurch and Canterbury

The Tasman River rises from the glaciers of the Alps, feeding into Lake Pukaki, the storage lake for the Upper Waitaki power scheme.

Mount Cook provides an imposing backdrop to the lake and the river.

The Legendary Land

The turquoise waters of the Tasman River are continually carving new channels in the dark river silt.

Christchurch and Canterbury

'Ki te tuohu koe me tuohu ki te maunga teitei.' 'If you must bow your head, let it be only to the highest mountain.'

Mount Cook is the King of New Zealand mountains, at 3,754 metres. The Maori name for the mountain is Aoraki, or Aorangi, variously translated as Cloud Piercer, Sky World, or Cloud in the Sky. This is, of course, the same Aorangi who travelled on the canoe of the gods to live on earth. When the canoe arrived it turned to stone and Aorangi, being the chief, became the tallest of all the gods petrified by the sun.

The Legendary Land

Christchurch and Canterbury

Mt Tasman, at 3,498 metres, is the second highest peak in Mt Cook National Park. There are, in fact, another 200 mountains in the Park that are higher than 2,500 metres.

The Legendary Land

At 29 kilometres in length, the Tasman Glacier is the longest in New Zealand. In earlier times it joined other glaciers to reach right down to the Mackenzie Basin.

The glacier is an astonishingly complex creation. At the top, sides and tributary joins there are crevasses, ice falls and ice fractures, which are constantly moving and creaking.

Christchurch and Canterbury

The road stretches on, past Twizel to Lindis Pass and the lake country of the south.

The Legendary Land

The West Coast

The most widely accepted Maori name for the South Island is Te Wai Pounamu, the place where the greenstone can be found.

It is this greenstone, or pounamu, that made the South Island so treasured by the Maori. This was the reason that North Island tribes battled over the northern part of the South Island. Whoever owned the greenstone trails owned the pounamu.

Greenstone is really a fish, which was owned by Ngahue, who lived in faraway Hawaiki. After being attacked by Sandstone Woman the fish fled with Ngahue to Aotearoa, where it found a home at Arahura on the West Coast. Some of the old people say that until you take the greenstone from the water it is still a fish. It turns to stone only because it is so angry at being caught.

There are many stories about treasured pieces of pounamu. Some people say that a greenstone which loses its shine is a premonition, a warning. Others say that a greenstone which has become separated from its rightful owner will swim back to them.

The West Coast is rather like a forest fortress, its mountain peaks palisades guarding against all-comers. A constant curtain of rain provides an extra layer of protection. Were it not for the fabled greenstone perhaps the Maori would never have come here, to the great Westland rivers, the Arahura and the Taramakau.

But come those sharp, still, spring days and 'the mountains with a full cloak of snow burn white against the sky, and the sunsets are acid-dream vivid, burnt orange and lime green, every shade of pink and maroon and scarlet with piles and bands of navy blue or silver clouds, and the sea gone weirdly pale jade. The lagoon will turn jet black, or abruptly fluoresce an unholy bright gold.' (Keri Hulme, *Homeplaces*, 1989.)

The Legendary Land

Later, another kind of stone, gold, brought Europeans into the area. Ironically, the gold was found beneath a greenstone boulder by Maori who were more interested in the pounamu. This was in 1864. A year later gold mining began in Hokitika and Reefton. Even later, another mineral, coal, added to the region's prosperity.

The goldmining days brought a sense of the frontier to the West Coast. Perhaps it is because of this that Coasters are considered different from other New Zealanders. Not any better or worse, just a bit different — irreverent, enterprising, sometimes stubborn, but always decent. In many respects they are the archetypal 'good keen men' and independent women of New Zealand's ideal society, having a healthy disrespect for authority and relying more on their own sense of what's right and what isn't.

Today the West Coast seems to exist outside of time. One of its most dominant features is the opalescent and eternal sea, which seems to carry on a constant love affair with the coast. Booming, roaring, whispering, cooing, gasping and sighing, the sea sings an ever-changing song of requited and unrequited love. Indeed, the whole of the West Coast is a place of whispers, of sounds and mysteries, offering moments of sheer beauty as when a white heron feathers the air at its nesting place at Okarito.

It is also a place of immense silence. The beaches are unpopulated and the emerald green forests are isolated. Nowhere is the silence more profound than at the two rivers of ice — the Fox and Franz Josef Glaciers. Sometimes, in the gleaming half-light of day, they defy reality and render the surrounding landscape unreal also.

In this lies the West Coast's secret. It is never what it seems to be and, sometimes, it is everything that it seems to be.

Water is a constant presence on the Coast, creating majestic falls and lush growth.

The West Coast

The Pancake Rocks at Punakaiki form the focal point of Paparoa National Park, south of Westport. The Park also encompasses stunning canyons, limestone formations and caves, all clothed with splendid flora and fauna tipped with the rich red of pohutukawa flowers.

The Legendary Land

Near Harihari a plantation of slender flax forms a foreground of light green needles against the darker forest.

The West Coast

At Okarito, like so many other places on the West Coast, you seem to be alone with the beach, the mountains and the endless sky.

The Legendary Land

Okarito was once a place where miners rushed to look for gold. Between 1868 and 1907 it was a town of pubs, dance halls, casinos, banks and stores, all doing great business. It may be quieter to look at now, but they still know how to live hard and drink hard. Just about the only thing out of place is the Abel Tasman monument; you can tell it's a recent addition designed by somebody from out of town. As for the rest, it's all in keeping, right?

The West Coast

The Legendary Land

New Zealand's Keri Hulme transformed the history of New Zealand literature when she won the Booker Prize with her novel *the bone people*. A permanent resident of Okarito, she is respected in a place where you take people as they are.

The West Coast

A lone canoeist on Okarito Lagoon, Westland National Park, is a lucky observer of nature's own son et lumière — the legendary aurora australis which floods the southern skies with light.

Near the lagoon, on the banks of the Waitangiroto Stream, is the only breeding ground of the kotuku, the stately white heron.

Kotuku have always been regarded with awe by the Maori because of their rarity, loveliness and grace in flight. Legend says that you should see the white heron at least once in a lifetime, thus 'He kotuku rerenga tahi', a white heron of a single flight. Kotuku were sometimes regarded as messengers of the spirit world.

The Legendary Land

The West Coast

The West Coasters are renowned for their stubborn individuality, well at home in the rugged landscape.

The Legendary Land

Goldpanner Norrie Groves continues to pan for gold at Gillespies Beach long after the gold rush days have gone.

The West Coast

Morning light, Lake Matheson, Westland National Park.

The Legendary Land

E maha nga rangi, ka tautau te remu, ka taikuiatia te whare.

When you get old your wrinkles will hang down and you will be an old woman around the house; so don't despise old age just because you are young right now.

The West Coast

Near the township of Fox Glacier there are wonderful views across Westland National Park to the mountains beyond. The Park lies between Greymouth and the Haast River.

Established in 1960, it contains 117,550 hectares extending from a wall of mountains to the Tasman Sea.

The Legendary Land

The cloud formations are nowhere more exciting than over the mountains, as here atop Fox Glacier.

The West Coast

The thick bush of the Coast provides endless opportunity for trampers, hunters and naturalists.

The Legendary Land

Peaceful Lake Moeraki is a favourite fishing spot. If you are very lucky you may see a white heron here.

The West Coast

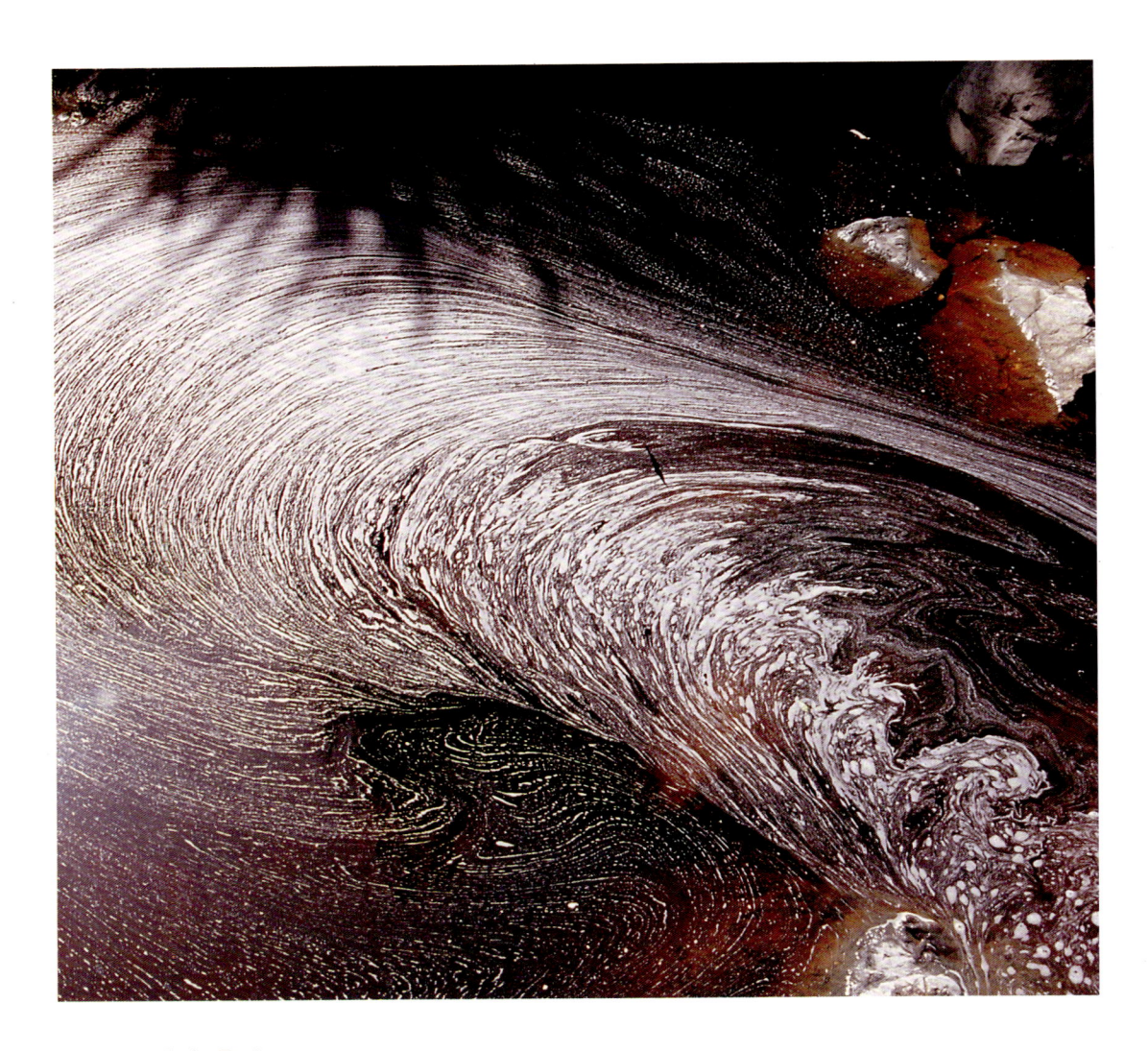

At Knight's Point, 40 kilometres from Haast, algae form a fascinating pattern on the surface of a stream.

The Legendary Land

The Maori people say, 'Mate atu he tete kura, whakaete mai he tete kura.' 'A fern frond dies, but another rises to take its place.'

The West Coast is the kingdom of ferns, from the minuscule umbrella fern to the wheki, the palm-like fern, and the tree fern.

Dunedin and Otago

Moa hunters were the first people to inhabit Otago, followed by the greenstone hunters, who trekked overland to the high Alps and the cold crystalline lakes to win the fabled stone from its jealous possessors. It is told that the whole interior was ruled over by kahui tipua, spirit protectors who could take the form of the rocks and mountains themselves.

The kahui tipua were most prominent at the place where Mount Aspiring stands, the highest point of Mount Aspiring National Park. To the south of Mount Aspiring is Lake Wakatipu. Some people say that it was in that place that the giant Matau, who had stolen a high-born Maori woman, was caught. His body was set on fire and when it was entirely consumed all that was left was the indentation and his still-living heart. It is this heart which makes the level of the lake rise and fall.

Today the grandeur of Otago still reflects those times when gods and the descendants of gods walked the earth. It is a place of mountains, lakes and glaciers. Most striking are The Remarkables, near Queenstown, but equally lovely are the mountains around Lakes Hawea, Wanaka and Wakatipu, where glaciers ground the hills into rounded shapes before the time of man. Then there is the Clutha, a river of immense strength, storming through steep gorges to the sea.

Queenstown is New Zealand's best-known mountain resort. An area of unsurpassable beauty, it is also a centre for adventure activities — jetboating, rafting, tramping, heliskiing or, for those who don't mind being tied by the ankles, the ultimate thrill — bungy jumping.

The earliest Europeans in Otago were whalers. As with Christchurch, however, settlers soon realised the potential of the alluvial plains, and in 1848 the ships *John Wickliffe* and *Philip Laing*, with three hundred settlers aboard, arrived in Otago Harbour. Primarily Presbyterian, the Scottish founders established Dunedin on the fortunes of great sheep stations. The discovery of gold

The Legendary Land

boosted the city's coffers and, by 1871, one in every four settlers in New Zealand was to be found in Otago. By the 1880s Dunedin was the country's largest, most industrialised and pre-eminent commercial city. Although this is not so today, Dunedin still exerts considerable influence nationally.

Dunedin has the reputation of being the Edinburgh of the South, the result of its Scottish heritage. Constructed of grey stone, it is a handsome city, with many buildings that are perfect Victorian artefacts. Everywhere there are church spires topping churches of austere Gothic grandeur. The Municipal Chambers display a frontage in the Italian style, while the architecture of the law courts, the railway station and the university attest to a Victorian exuberance muted by a sense of respectability.

Of the gracious houses on the Otago Peninsula and the Taieri Plains, none is grander than Olveston, a home built in the Jacobean style, or the imposing Larnach Castle, just outside the city.

Throughout Otago there are still signs of a prosperity based on whaling, sheep rearing and gold. Otago's greatest treasure, though, is its unique landscape — the rugged hills, piercing mountains, mighty rivers and gentle lakes — that fills its people with pride and captivates every visitor.

An albatross wheels above the Royal Albatross Colony at Taiaroa Head, on the Otago Peninsula.

Dunedin and Otago

Once a Maori track through the mountains, the Lindis Pass is the northern gateway connecting the stark Central Otago heights with the Mackenzie Country. The view from the Pass reveals tussock mountains, their tops eroded by the elements. Sometimes you will see a New Zealand falcon skirling its cry across the land.

The Legendary Land

Winter brings cold weather and often blizzard conditions to Otago, and both sheep and man have had to learn to meet the challenges of this awesome country.

Lake Hawea is a water-filled glaciated valley, the result of glacier action which has smoothed and rounded the landscape below the surrounding peaks.

The Maori say that Hawea and neighbouring Lake Wanaka were dug by Chief Te Rakaihautu using a huge digging stick. The rubble from his digging, piled high, has formed the surrounding mountains.

The Legendary Land

Lake Wanaka, 45 km long and 4.8 km at its widest, is larger than neighbouring Hawea. The lake and the small resort town of the same name attract thousands of visitors in summer and winter. The town is the headquarters of Mount Aspiring National Park.

Dunedin and Otago

The Legendary Land

Moonrise over the peaks of Mount Aspiring National Park.

It may come as a surprise but it is not a man up there in the moon but a woman. Her name, according to Maori legend, was Rona. One night she took a gourd and went to draw water from a spring. She stumbled when the moon went behind a cloud and swore at it. Angry, the moon came down from the sky and, although Rona held tight to a ngaio tree, the moon took her up with it, gourd, ngaio tree and all. This is why you should always remember what happened to Rona before you abuse anyone or anything.

Dunedin and Otago

The Matukituki Valley in Mt Aspiring National Park has always been a favourite with trampers.

The river is not always kind, and was named 'white destroyer' by the Maori.

The Legendary Land

'Get in behind, Skip!'
A river of sheep at Loch Linnhe Station as shepherds and dogs work together at mustering time. Loch Linnhe Station is one of many that link back to Central Otago's run-holding past and the sagas of the great High Country sheep stations.

Dunedin and Otago

Sheep are driven along the highway on the banks of Lake Wakatipu. Drovers, whistling instructions to their dogs, shepherd the flock to one side so that traffic may pass.

The Legendary Land

Dunedin and Otago

Vineyards sit incongruously beneath the rugged hills of the Kawarau Valley. This vineyard at Chard Farm is one of a growing number in Otago that are achieving widespread recognition.

The Legendary Land

Fed from the high alps of Mount Aspiring National Park, the brawling Kawarau River twists, turns and rushes through gorges and clefts of rock.

Dunedin and Otago

The sun pours a golden river of light across The Remarkables near Queenstown. In the foreground is the Kawarau River.

The Legendary Land

TSS *Earnslaw* is the only survivor of four steamers which plied Lake Wakatipu during the height of the gold rush days.

Dunedin and Otago

Queenstown at night. The glowing lights beneath the pale mountains are like the underground domain of Ruaumoko, god of earthquakes, volcanoes and subterranean fires.

The Legendary Land

Set on the shores of Lake Wakatipu, Queenstown has one of the most dramatic locations in the world. Once part of a sheep run, Queenstown soon became caught up in the gold rushes. Today it is a popular resort town, providing a lively centre for the area's skiing and adventure activities.

Dunedin and Otago

The Moeraki coastline is steeped in Maori history. The famed Moeraki boulders, each weighing several tonnes, are said to be the petrified food baskets of the *Araiteuru* canoe which was wrecked on the offshore reef. Early whalers, with other imagery in mind, called them the Ninepins.

The Legendary Land

Dunedin and Otago

A sea lion, glistening sovereign of the seashore, roars at Moeraki Peninsula.

The Legendary Land

Moeraki, 78 kilometres north of Dunedin, is today a tiny fishing hamlet.

Dunedin and Otago

The Legendary Land

The land gentles as it nears the coast. Sheep search for sustenance through a thin mantle of snow near Middlemarch, Central Otago.

Dunedin and Otago

The University of Otago was the first to be opened in New Zealand. The old part of the university, built in the 1870s, has some similarities to the University of Glasgow.

Dunedin has many fine old buildings. Olveston, at 42 Royal Terrace, is an Edwardian residence that was built between 1904 and 1906. The house conjures up the elegance of a bygone era, beautifully embellished with antiques and memorabilia. The staircase is Jacobean in style.

The Legendary Land

Dunedin railway station, built in 1907, is a resplendent palace complete with a mosaic floor, stained-glass windows and a soaring, copper-domed tower.

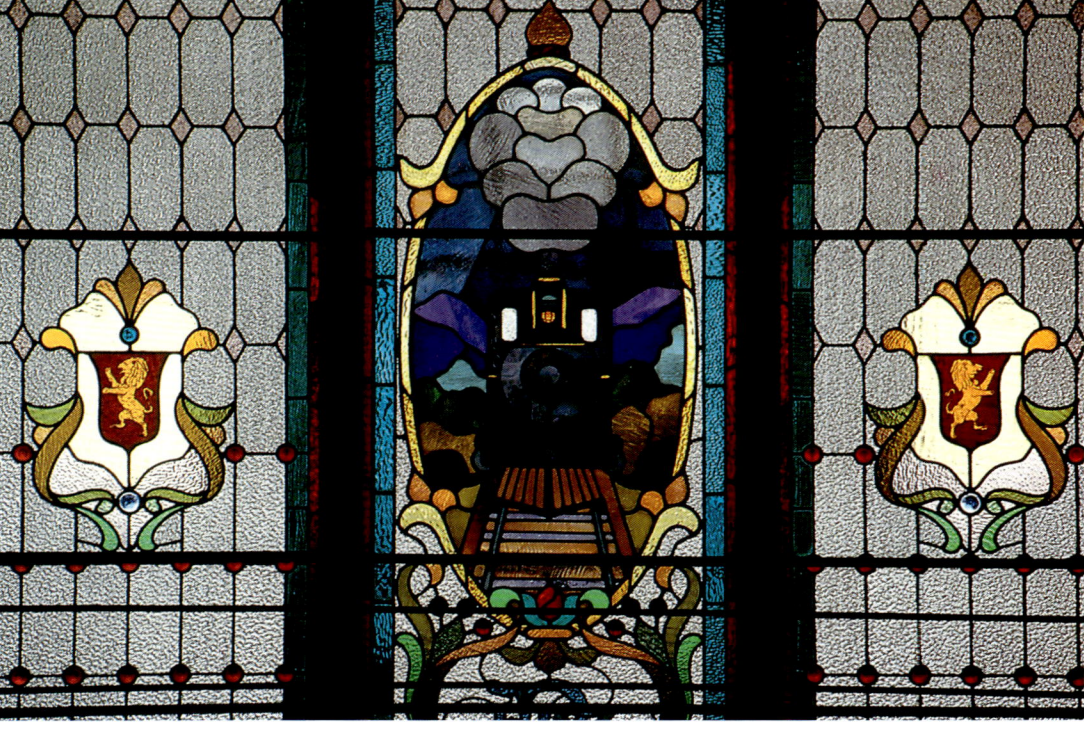

195

Murihiku: The South

So we come to Murihiku, the tail end of the land. It must have been cold and forbidding for those barely clothed Maori voyagers, but they journeyed even this far south. First the Waitaha, then the Ngati Mamoe and finally the Ngai Tahu. It must also have been cold for those Europeans who came to harvest seals and chase whales.

Murihiku encompasses Southland, Fiordland and Stewart Island. Southland's history is similar to that of Otago. Invercargill was settled by Scots people from Dunedin in 1856, and the Scots heritage is still noticeable in the way Southlanders speak; there is a distinct burr on their r's. The new settlers found Southland similar to the Scottish highlands, and they established sheep runs on the Southland plains.

Bluff is the harbour from which agricultural produce is sent to all parts of the globe. It is also a vigorous fishing port, with catches of deep-sea fish, crayfish and shellfish. The Bluff oyster is considered by connoisseurs to be the ultimate in oysters.

Offshore from Invercargill is Stewart Island, a special place of bush-clad hills and quiet beaches. The Maori name is Rakiura, a reference to the glowing skies and auroras which play on the southern horizon.

West of Invercargill the vista opens out to the unparalleled beauty of Fiordland National Park. This is the carved stern of Te Waka o Aoraki, the canoe of the gods. Sea and the massive forces of the Ice Ages have weathered the intricate carvings but have also created astounding physical configurations to the land. Every day rain, wind, cloud and sleet combine to recreate an ever-changing panorama. Along the coast are the great fiords — Milford, Bligh, Caswell, Nancy, Doubtful, Dusky and Preservation Inlet. Inland are the Taki-timu Mountains and the lakes Te Anau and Manapouri.

From Te Anau you can take the magnificent Milford Track, a walk which

The Legendary Land

has been called the finest in the world. The route takes you through fabulous forests, past waterfalls and alongside mountain peaks to Milford Sound itself.

Here, man is but a tiny speck against the magnitude of Nature. Here, as nowhere else, the supernatural surrounds you — in the waterfalls cascading from cliffs into deep Sounds below; in the lakes, sprawled beneath the enormous mountains. The world that the Maori voyagers had heard about in far off Hawaiki ends in this place of mystery and glacial beauty. If ever there was a Lost World, Fiordland is it.

It is said that one of the canoes of the Maori voyagers, the *Takitimu*, is now hidden within a subterranean chamber of the Takitimu Mountains. But who knows? Perhaps some intrepid adventurers ventured even further, toward the Antarctic continent.

It is also said that it was to Milford Sound that the fantail which had laughed when Maui tried to conquer death came to do penance for its act.

So we are back to Maui, the great demi-god, who started it all by fishing up Aotearoa. As it came rearing out of the waves, the water streamed away from it, uncovering its beauty and greatness.

For the first time the sun flashed upon it.

Aotearoa.

It awaits.

The legendary land.

Mitre Peak rises above Milford Sound, chiselling the sky.

Murihiku: The South

The area about Milford Sound was revered by the Maori as the place where the greenstone known as tangiwai could be found. Some say that the tears within the stone came from the fantail which laughed when Maui tried to conquer Lady Death, Hine nui te Po. Others say that the tears are those of Tama, who had come to Aotearoa seeking his three wives. On his arrival he found that because of a transgression they had all been turned to greenstone. In this version, the tangiwai is one of the wives and the black water drops within the greenstone are the tears which Tama shed when he found his greenstone wife.

The Legendary Land

The road to Milford passes the Mirror Lakes, with their view across to Ngatimamoe Peak, sacred mountain of the Ngatimamoe tribe.

Murihiku: The South

Mitre Peak, Milford Sound.

The Legendary Land

Ahakoa he iti ra, he iti mapihi pounamu.

Although it may be small, it is precious like the greenstone.

Murihiku: The South

The sheer walls that rise above Milford Sound are cut with cascading waterfalls. The constant mist is a sign that Papa, the Earth Mother, is mourning her husband Rangi, the Sky Father above.

The Legendary Land

Water snakes out from the steaming cauldron at the base of the Sterling Falls.

Murihiku: The South

On the Milford Track, magnificent views contrast with the closeness of the primeval bush.

The Legendary Land

Maori people have always considered the rainbow to be one of the most potent of omens. When seen on the right the auguries were good. When seen on the left, they were bad. A pale rainbow signified death. Sometimes the rainbow formed a bridge between the real world and the spirit world.

Here the Bowen Falls leap through a rainbow to the valley floor below.

205

Murihiku: The South

The Legendary Land

Lake Manapouri is often regarded as New Zealand's most beautiful lake. It has an atmosphere of reflective, brooding power. Its present name evokes 'the heart that sorrows'; its original name was Moturau, lake of a hundred islands.

Murihiku: The South

Early morning mist, Doubtful Sound.

The Legendary Land

Ki te hamama popoia te tangata, e kore e mau te ika.

If a man spends his nights yawning he will never catch any fish.

Murihiku: The South

The Legendary Land

Fiordland National Park is one of the last great wildernesses. At 1.2 million hectares, its area is greater than that of all the other national parks of New Zealand combined.

Fiordland encompasses over a dozen fabulous fiords. Doubtful Sound was named 'Doubtfull Harbour' by Captain Cook in 1770 because he was unsure that his ship would be able to enter and exit the somewhat narrow entrance.

211

Murihiku: The South

The Legendary Land

The Acheron Passage is named after the survey ship *Acheron*, which undertook a hydrological survey of Fiordland in 1850. The ship's captain was profoundly moved by the 'towering cliffs which dwindled the *Acheron*'s masts into nothing.'

Murihiku: The South

The Legendary Land

A derelict shed is made golden by the morning sun, near Clifden in Southland.

Although only about five percent of New Zealand's population live here, Southland produces twenty percent of the country's agricultural produce.

Murihiku: The South

Low tide, Oreti Beach, Southland.

The Legendary Land

Waiho ma te tangata e mihi.

Let others praise you.

Murihiku: The South

Until Bluff was established as a port, sailing ships and steamers often sailed up the Oreti River right to Invercargill. Today Oreti Beach is a superb place to walk, fossick for driftwood and shells, and swim.

Across the water lies Stewart Island, known to the Maori as Rakiura, island of glowing skies.

The Legendary Land

In some of the old stories, Rakiura is the anchorstone of Maui's canoe. When he fished up the land he needed the anchorstone to take the strain of such a large fish.

The Maori have always come here to harvest the smaller offshore islands for the titi or muttonbird, and today Stewart Island supports a vigorous fishing industry.

Epilogue

Kia hora te marino,

kia whakapapa pounamu te moana

kia tere te karohirohi

i mua i tou huarahi.

May the calm be widespread,

may the surface of the ocean

glisten like greenstone,

and may the shimmer of sunlight

ever dance across your pathway.

The Legendary Land

Photographic Notes

The photographs in this book were taken with the following equipment:

Leica M6 with 1:2.0/35 and 1:1.4/75 Summicron-M lenses.
Nikon F90 and F801s with 1:2.8/20, 1:3.3/24-50, 1:2.8/105 Macro, and 1:2.8/80-200 AF Nikkor lenses, along with a Nikon Speedlight SB-24 flash.
Widelux F8 panorama camera.
Bogen 3221 tripod — heavy, bulky, yet invaluable.

The images were photographed on Fujichrome RDP-100 Professional Film, which was processed by Faulkner Color Lab in San Francisco, California.

Acknowledgements

Special thanks to: Anne Leue (for many enjoyable hours at the light table), Jo Downey of the New Zealand Tourism Board office in Frankfurt (for her encouragement right from the start), *GLOBO — Das Reisemagazin* (for the fabulous assignments).

For their generous support, thanks to Ansett New Zealand, Fiordland Travel, Maui Campas and The Regent of Auckland.

Thanks also to Air New Zealand International; AJ Hackett Bungy Jumping, Queenstown; Awaroa Lodge & Cafe, Abel Tasman National Park; Bay of Islands Aero Club, Kerikeri; Blackwater Rafting Tours, Waitomo; Brian Boru Hotel, Thames; Bridge to Nowhere Jet, Whanganui National Park; Doug Johansen's Adventure Treks, Pauanui; Driving Creek Railway, Coromandel; Fox Glacier Helicopters; Fullers Northland, Paihia; Gannet Beach Adventures, Cape Kidnappers; Huka Lodge, Taupo; Kelly Tarlton's Underwater World, Auckland; Loch Linnhe Station, Queenstown; Milford Track Guided Walk, Te Anau; Mountain Air, Tongariro National Park; New Zealand Tourism Board, Wellington; NZ Maori Arts & Crafts Institute, Rotorua; Okarito Nature Tours; Okarito YHA; Opoutere YHA; Puka Park Lodge, Pauanui; Ruatoki School; Ruapehu Skotel; Sheraton Rotorua; Southern Air, Invercargill; Southern Lakes Helicopters, Milford Sound; Stewart Island Travel; Taieri Gorge Railroad, Dunedin; Tarawera Helicopters, Rotorua; Tekapo Air Safaris; The Helicopter Line, Auckland, Mt Cook and Queenstown; Vulcan Helicopters, Whakatane; and Whale Watch Kaikoura Ltd.

The Legendary Land

For the great times, thanks to friends and fellow travellers Thomas Keidel, Sigrid Schott-Keidel, Anke Janik, Michael Butler, John Adams, Fiona McKinnon, Scott Scheigis, Julie Digby, Dennis Holberg, Mette Gaarde, Ady Illingworth, Manuela Drobner, Martin McGurk, Tom Appleton, Tanja Blinkhorn, Andrew Ewens, Michael Markewitsch, Monika Markewitsch, Armin Tränker, Regina Tränker and Tracy Jackson.

Thank you, Keri Hulme.

Thank you, Moengaroa Kerei and family.

Thank you, Ian Watt.

For taking care of business in San Francisco, thank you Doug Dirks, Igal Dahari, Matt Brocchini.

And thank you, Meredith Garlick and Kevin Griffith, for introducing me to the Southern Hemisphere.

— H.L.

Thanks to Montana Wines Ltd and Air New Zealand for travel assistance in the South Island, and to Holger Leue, Keri Hulme, Ian Watt, Susan Brierley, Chris Lipscombe, Alison Jacobs and the *Legendary Land* iwi.

— V.I.

Also by Holger Leue:

Epiphyllum — The Splendor of Leaf Cacti (1987)

Also by Witi Ihimaera:

Pounamu, Pounamu (1972)
Tangi (1973)
Whanau (1974)
The New Net Goes Fishing (1977)
Into the World of Light (ed. with D.S. Long, 1982)
The Matriarch (1986)
The Whale Rider (1987)
Dear Miss Mansfield (1989)
Te Ao Marama (ed., 5 volumes, 1992–)